The Taos Pueblo
and Its Sacred Blue Lake

The Taos Pueblo
and Its Sacred Blue Lake

Marcia Keegan

Foreword by Stewart L. Udall

CLEAR LIGHT PUBLISHERS, SANTA FE

Clear Light Publishers, 823 Don Diego, Santa Fe, N.M. 87501

First Edition

Library of Congress Cataloging-in-Publication Data
Keegan, Marcia
    Taos Pueblo and Its Sacred Blue Lake / Marcia Keegan : foreword by
Stewart L. Udall.
                p.   cm.
    Includes bibliographical references and index.
    ISBN 0-940666-12-X : $14.95
    1. Taos Indians — History. 2. Taos Indians — Land tenure. 3. Taos
Pueblo (N.M.) I. Title.
E99.T2K43 1991
978.9'53 —dc20   91-72482
                                       CIP

Designed by Irving Warhaftig
Typography by Michael Picón

Printed in MEXICO

Front Cover: Victory Celebration at Taos Pueblo, 1971

All royalties from the sale of this book are being donated to the Oo-oonah Children's Art Center at Taos Pueblo.

Dedicated to all my friends at Taos Pueblo

Foreword

"In the dust where we have buried the silent races and their abominations, we have buried so much of the delicate magic of life."

D.H. Lawrence (at Taos)

THE STORY of the long battle fought by the Taos Indians to regain Blue Lake, a sacred shrine nestled in a beautiful pine forest high in the Sangre de Cristo Mountains of New Mexico, is the story of a triumph of the human spirit. It is also a story which dramatizes the deep, abiding attachment American Indians have for parts of the earth that have been intertwined with their lives and their religious ceremonies for centuries. As a participant in this struggle in the 1960s, I would like to believe that the restoration of Blue Lake to the ownership and stewardship of the Taos Indians marks a turning point in American history. Until the last half of this century, the leaders of our nation exhibited little sensitivity to Indian art, to the "delicate magic" generated by Indian ceremonies and religious practices, or to the land wisdom expressed in Indian attitudes toward the earth and its resources. One of the strange twists of the fight over Blue Lake is that it was our first great conservation president, Theodore Roosevelt, who signed the order in 1906 that ignored the rights of the Taos Indians and converted their sacred ground into a *national* forest owned by all Americans. For decades, the reversal of this decision appeared to be a hopeless cause to everyone except the religious leaders of Taos Pueblo. To most conservationists, once land was designated as a national forest or a national park it became, for them, a different kind of "sacred" ground — and many of these well-meaning Americans became vigorous opponents of the effort to restore Blue Lake to the Indians from whom it was taken. In the end, a hopeless cause became a winning cause when the Taos leaders refused to accept defeat after defeat and finally persuaded the Congress that Blue Lake *was* their sacred ground, and if it were returned to their stewardship it would be conserved with a love and care that the federal government could not match. This splendid story deserves endless retelling. It is, indeed, a sign of American maturity that today the conservation movement finds itself, guided by ecological insights, turning back to the Indian idea that we are not outside of nature, but of it.

Stewart L. Udall
Santa Fe, 1991

Taos Pueblo Return of Blue Lake Commemorative Committee; left to right Teresino Jiron, Tony Reyna, Al Lujan, Gilbert Suazo, Fred Romero, and Vincente Lujan.

THE PATIENCE and persistence of the Taos Elders has resulted in the return of Blue Lake to the people of Taos Pueblo. Today we can celebrate, knowing the sacred area is finally ours. We can also celebrate the many days and nights to come, knowing that the work of our Elders will always be an example of what spirit and devotion will mean to our little ones.

Tony Reyna
Chairman, Taos Pueblo Return of Blue Lake
Commemorative Committee and
former governor, Taos Pueblo

The Taos Pueblo
and Its Sacred Blue Lake

HIGH IN THE MOUNTAINS of northern New Mexico lies a deep cool lake the color of sparkling turquoise. The water from mountain springs collects here in this lake surrounded by pines. In the lake the water grows still, reflecting the crystal sky, before it pours out once more in a stream. Splashing and churning over and around rocks, the water eventually reaches a plateau 4,000 feet below the mountaintops, where it flows rapidly through a broad plaza in the middle of an adobe village. This village, or pueblo, with its two earth colored terraces rising stairstep fashion on either side of the stream, is the home of the Taos Indians. The stream is the Rio Pueblo, and its source is their sacred Blue Lake, known to them as "Ma-wha-lo."

The Taos Indians have always believed that the waters of Blue Lake are the source of all life for them, and the final resting place for their souls after death. Blue Lake is, for the Taos Indians, equivalent to St. Peter's in Rome, the temple in Jerusalem, or the holy mosque in Mecca. Every year for centuries the Taos Indians have made a pilgrimage to the shores of Blue Lake, where they hold religious ceremonies only their tribe may attend.

Quirino Romero

Quirino Romero, a leader of the tribe, said, "Blue Lake for our life is living. Blue Lake is where the spirit of Indian God is still living today. We go over there to pray, and we go over there to worship. The stars and the moon and the sun and the sky and the clouds and the air and whatever nature has provided for us, we do believe in this."

According to legend, Taos Pueblo was founded by a great chief who, following an eagle, led his people up a stream to the foot of the mountains. In the place where the eagle dropped two plumes, one falling on either side of a stream, the Indians built their permanent home.

Taos Pueblo has been continuously inhabited for around 800 years, according to historians and archaeologists. It was probably already 400 years old when the Spanish arrived in 1540. Seeing the Indians of the area in their towering villages, *pueblos* in Spanish, the explorers called them Pueblo Indians. Early descriptions of Taos Pueblo suggest that it has changed little in appearance since that time.

Taos Pueblo lies at the foot of Mount Wheeler, tallest
peak in the Sangre de Cristo mountain range.

A rider on the Rio Pueblo, which flows down from Blue Lake.

King Charles I of Spain pronounced New Mexico a Spanish province in 1689, granting tracts of land to each of the Indian pueblos. Taos retained title to its sacred Blue Lake. And these Spanish land grants were recognized by Mexico after that nation gained its independence from Spain. Although they adopted Christianity, the Pueblo Indians never abandoned their original beliefs, and the Taos Indians continued to worship at Blue Lake as they had always done. When the United States acquired New Mexico in 1848 under the Treaty of Guadalupe Hidalgo, it pledged to honor all property rights in the Territory.

In 1906, however, all these guarantees were rescinded by the United States. In that year, President Theodore Roosevelt established Taos National Forest (now Carson National Forest) as a public recreation area. The new national forest included 50,000 acres of Taos Indian land, together with Blue Lake; and there was no provision for compensation to the Taos Indians. At first the Taos Indians, after being promised that the Blue Lake area would be off-limits to anyone but themselves, agreed to the establishment of this national forest. But this promise was quickly broken. Soon logging roads provided access to the area, and other evidence of Anglo culture, such as beer bottles and paper trash, appeared in Blue Lake. It was no longer possible to conduct their sacred rites in secrecy, and ritual objects placed by Indians near the site were maliciously or carelessly destroyed by the public. The sanctity of the Indians' holy shrine was destroyed.

Shortly after these events, the Taos Indians began a long struggle to have their sacred Blue Lake returned to them. The story of this struggle is one of the most remarkable tales in the annals of the complex and often tortured relations between the federal government and the American Indians, from whom it seized the land we now call the United States.

The History of Taos Pueblo
Ancient Indian History

I T IS BELIEVED that the Tiwa-speaking inhabitants of Taos Pueblo are perhaps descendants of the Mesa Verde people. Sometime during the thirteenth century, severe droughts probably caused these people to abandon the Mesa Verde region and wander, seeking new, more fertile land. It is likely that they built other adobe pueblos along the way, inhabiting them for a time and eventually migrating slowly towards the Sangre de Cristo Mountains.

Traces of such settlements are scattered throughout the Taos Valley. Ruins of dwellings, as well as pictographs, petroglyphs, and other archaeological evidence tell of old villages and ceremonial grounds. Stone arrowheads, tools, and pottery shards are often found in the area. Some shards dating from the fourteenth century have been discovered at Taos Pueblo, but it is not known exactly when the pueblo was founded.

The adobe pueblo, often called "the original apartment building," is the only indigenous architectural form unique to North America. As is the custom today, Taos Pueblo was originally built of stacked mud and straw adobe bricks, rather than mud and straw adobe piled on in layers. Wood vigas, or beams, supported earthen roofs that were

Pete Concha and grandchild.

James Mirabel with his granddaughter Rosemarie Cordova
and great-granddaughter Jana Cordova.

sometimes covered with grass. The pueblo may have been, as it is today, five or six stories high. The pyramidal shape is created by making each higher story smaller than the one below it by the width of a room. In the old days, when defense was the primary function of the structure, residents entered by climbing a ladder to the roof and slipping through an opening in the roof to the room below. With thick walls devoid of doors and windows, the original pueblo probably looked more like a fort than a dwelling place.

Today only Taos Pueblo, out of all the nineteen pueblos in New Mexico, has retained its fortress-like appearance. Doors and windows have been cut into the walls on every level, but the upper stories may still be reached by ladder. Modern Taos Indians still spend a great deal of time caring for and refurbishing the pueblo structure, since otherwise, like all adobe, it would disintegrate due to the action of rain and ground water. Roofs and boards must be patched regularly, and often the work is undertaken communally or in family groups. Replastering is a frequent chore. Every year a fresh layer of adobe is applied, often by the women, who have developed great skill in handling the mud; traditionally, the exterior surface texture is created with a sheepskin.

The Coming of the Spanish

WHEN FRANCISCO CORONADO arrived in the area in 1540, Pueblo culture was flourishing, and a chronicler who traveled with Coronado, Pedro de Castaneda, wrote admiringly of the level of civilization that the people had attained. In 1598, Juan de Oñate arrived and established his first capital on the Rio Grande less than fifty miles down river from Taos Pueblo. This more permanent intrusion by the Spanish was to bring about major changes in Pueblo life. As elsewhere in lands conquered by Spain, the Indians were forced to provide free labor, food, and supplies to their colonial masters. Spanish priests seeking Christian converts went out to the pueblos, and any resistance to Spanish secular authority was quickly punished by death or slavery. The Indians had probably always guarded their mysteries tightly, but the arrival of the Spanish made secrecy important to their very survival. After a brief uprising at Acoma was violently punished, the Pueblo Indians' overt resistance subsided.

Throughout the first part of the seventeenth century, the Spanish moved gradually into New Mexico, settling primarily along the Rio Grande, near their capital town of Santa Fe. By 1670, around 2,800 Spaniards lived in the Rio Grande Valley; a few also lived on haciendas to the north, where they farmed and raised sheep. By far the most significant Spanish activity in the area was the effort to convert Indians to Christianity, and many friars and officials worked hard to eradicate all traces of the original native beliefs. Pueblo medicine men, their "competition," were violently suppressed by the Spanish. But the Indians, even those who professed Catholicism, apparently worked secretly to sustain their own belief system and ceremonies.

The Pueblo Revolt

IN 1675, the Spanish governor, Juan Francisco Trevino, learned of a scheduled meeting of medicine men. He dispatched troops to their meeting site and arrested forty-seven of them. After executing three, he released the others with a strong warning not to continue their meetings and practices.

One of the medicine men who survived was Popé, from San Juan Pueblo. When he returned home, Spanish surveillance of him continued, and he ultimately fled to Taos Pueblo, where support for him was strong. During the following years, Popé and other Indians planned what was to be known as the Pueblo Revolt. Popé spoke to the Taos Indians about powerful spirits who had visited him in the kiva and had given him the inspiration for such plans. The attack plan that the Indians proposed was designed to completely eradicate Spanish presence in New Mexico.

Eventually many separate pueblos joined the alliance to eradicate Spanish domination. It was, at that time, the most complete pueblo alliance in recorded history. The revolt was scheduled to begin

Frank Romero, Taos Pueblo, 1971.

A kiva at Taos Pueblo.

in many locations simultaneously at dawn on a specific day in August 1680. It would require the cooperation of many thousands of Indians from different tribes, speaking different languages, and scattered over an area of thousands of miles. As a means of keeping track of the days remaining until the revolt was scheduled to begin, runners were sent to all participating tribes carrying knotted cords. One knot was to be untied each day, and when no knots were left, all Indian groups would rise up against the Spanish. Planning this attack and keeping it secret for so long and among so many people scattered over so great an area required remarkable unity and trust.

Unfortunately, just two days before the revolt was to begin, two captured Indian messengers gave the plan away to the Spanish. When the Indians learned that their secret had been revealed, they decided to begin the revolt immediately. Runners were sent out to all pueblos to inform them, and the uprising began by the dawn of August 10. Spanish losses were great, and the few survivors hastened towards Santa Fe, where they clustered inside the walls of the town. Outside, the Indians laid siege to the town, and managed to cut off its water supply. Eventually the Spanish were able to disperse the Indians long enough to prepare their own retreat south, leaving Santa Fe on August 21, 1680. They were not to return to New Mexico for twelve years.

The Spanish who later returned to Santa Fe were led by a new governor, Don Diego de Vargas. They attempted a conciliatory approach to the Indians, and were met with tentative pledges of friendship. But mistrust of the Spanish persisted, and the Indians made sporadic efforts to resist, including a short-lived attempt in 1696 to repeat their triumph of 1680. Each time, however, Indian resistance was overcome by Spanish military force, and eventually the two groups settled into an uneasy truce, with the Taos Indians guardedly promising to cooperate. The Pueblo country was once again a province of New Spain, subject to the rule of the Spanish empire; and the Catholics continued their missionary work.

Moonrise over the church at Taos Pueblo.

Historic bell tower of San Geronimo.

The Revolt of 1847

THE NEXT MAJOR revolt against Spanish rule took place in 1836, and it also began at Taos, although the headquarters was soon moved to Santa Cruz. This time, the issue was the unpopularity of the governor newly appointed by the Mexican president. The governor, Colonel Albino Perez, further exacerbated his difficulties by levying new taxes shortly after taking office. This time both the Spaniards and the Indians joined together in the uprising, led by General Chopon of Taos. After quickly defeating the governor, the combined Spanish and Indian forces called a general assembly to elect their own governor, José Gonzales of Taos; Gonzales's mother was a Taos Pueblo Indian, and his father was half Indian.

However, this new popular government coalition was not to endure. It was very shortly betrayed by one of its Spanish founders, Manuel Armijo, who summoned troops from the Mexican garrison to assist him in a counterattack. When the Indian Governor Gonzales approached his former ally in friendship, Armijo immediately captured him and had him shot. Once again, New Mexico's pueblos were to be ruled by a foreign power — the Mexican government.

This Mexican dominion did not last long. The personal rule of Armijo, the usurper, ended after his second term, when the United States Army, victor in the war with Mexico, invaded New Mexico in 1846. Armijo fled, and the advancing troops arrived unopposed in Santa Fe, where Charles Bent was soon installed as United States Territorial Governor. Immediately, resistance to United States control began, initiated, once again, by Taos Indians. The badly organized revolt of 1847 was the result. Governor Bent was assassinated, and his death was immediately punished by the United States Army, which pursued 700 of the rebels into Taos Pueblo's church, San Geronimo.

In the fighting that followed, the thatched roof of the church was set on fire and, as flaming rafters fell on the Indians inside, the adobe building itself was hacked by axes and pummeled by heavy artillery. Finally, the wall of the church was opened, and as the United States Army rushed inside, many Indians fled toward the mountains. However, the United States Cavalry continued to engage the Indians in combat, and looking back toward their pueblo, the Indians suddenly saw the walls of San Geronimo collapse. They took this as an omen and surrendered. Many Indians had died in the fighting, the pueblo church was totally destroyed, and six leaders of the revolt were tried and hanged. The ruins of old San Geronimo can still be seen today, a reminder of this tragic event in the history of Taos Pueblo.

Ruins of San Geronimo at Taos Pueblo graveyard.

The Rio Pueblo, which flows down from Blue Lake, was traditionally the main source of water for the pueblo.

Land and Water Rights Issues

THE ORIGINAL Spanish land grants, assented to by the United States Government after its acquisition of New Mexico Territory, reserved large tracts of land for the pueblos. This land was to be held communally rather than individually by each pueblo, in trust for its members. But an early United States court ruling ignored these provisions and permitted the sale of land by individual Indians to non-Indians. By the time this ruling was reversed by the United States Supreme Court in 1913, a considerable amount of pueblo land had fallen into the hands of non-Indians, often by illegal means. The Secretary of the Interior, Albert B. Fall, engaged in legislative efforts to resolve, in favor of non-Indians, any questionable titles to illegally obtained Indian land. The proposed legislation, introduced by Senator Bursum and known as the Bursum Bill, would have further curtailed Indian land and water rights. The Bureau of Indian Affairs supported the bill, and probably it would

have passed if John Collier and other sympathetic non-Indians had not alerted the Pueblos to its ghastly implications.

This impending threat revived the activities of the All Indian Pueblo Council, after 250 years of nonaction. A delegation was sent to Washington to oppose the bill, and emissaries were sent to other Indian organizations to arouse united opposition. In response, the Bureau of Indian Affairs then passed local legislation outlawing Taos religious practices and social gatherings, unless approved by the bureau.

Fortunately, these attempts at repression were unsuccessful; the Bursum Bill was defeated and replaced with legislation permitting the Indians to settle their own land questions. But the Bureau of Indian Affairs did not give up easily, and in a further move of retribution, it arrested the entire Taos Council of Elders on charges related to the Taos practice of taking young boys out of public school during the time of their

initiation into manhood in the kivas. The federal district judge rebuked the bureau and ordered the men released. As Indians all over the nation moved to take into their own hands issues concerning their lands, water rights, tribal governments, and the education of their youth, Indian affairs began to improve. One signal of the beginning of this new era in New Mexico was the appointment of John Collier, one of the non-Indian opponents of the Bursum Bill, as the new Indian Commissioner.

The Government of Taos Pueblo

TAOS PUEBLO is, and has been for as long as history relates, self-governing. At the beginning of each year, an election is held to select the tribal governor, lieutenant governor, and other officers. Together with members of the Tribal Council, these individuals determine policy for tribal civic affairs. Other members of the council include religious officers and the tribal elders, the older men. The governor, who serves as tribal spokesman, is assisted by a tribal interpreter and carries four canes as symbols of his office. One cane was given to the pueblo in 1620 by the king of Spain; another was a gift from President Abraham Lincoln on the occasion of a Taos governor's visit to Washington in 1863; the third was given to the pueblo by New Mexico Governor Bruce King in 1980; and the fourth was presented by King Carlos of Spain in 1987.

One of the pueblo officers elected each year is the war chief, whose responsibilities include internal affairs and forest husbandry. Today's "war" is more likely to be fought against forest fires, and today's "warriors" are Taos's fire fighting crews, the celebrated "Snowballs." The name was inspired when snow, which to Indians represents a blessing of the spirits, fell heavily once when the fire fighters had just finished putting out a fire in the Lincoln National Forest. Overseeing relations between the United States Forest Service and the Taos fire fighters is one of the major duties of the war chief, whose fire fighting tools stand outside his door throughout his term, as symbols of his office.

Another important tribal leader is the cacique, the spiritual and ceremonial officer. The same man holds this office throughout his life, and after his death, it is passed on to the next generation in his family. This office requires intense training throughout the officer's youth, and the complete devotion of all his time as an adult. Under the cacique are the kiva chiefs, who preside over the six kivas, secret halls of initiation and ritual that are the center of the tribe's ceremonial life and religious education.

Tribal officials at the Blue Lake celebration, August 1971, were (left to right) the religious and
spiritual leader Juan de Jesús Romero, Lieutenant Governor Pete Concha, and Governor John Reyna.

Daily Life at Taos Pueblo

THE TAOS PEOPLE have been farmers from time immemorial. Evidence of crop growing has been found at very ancient prehistoric sites in the Southwest, and some of the plants cultivated then — corn, beans, pumpkin, and squash — are still grown at Taos today. These days there are also apple and plum trees, as well as livestock. Horses, cattle, sheep, and a small herd of buffalo graze on the grasslands around the reservation.

Long known for the quality of their drums and their moccasins, the Taos Indians still make and sell traditional

A traditional horno (outdoor oven) is used for baking bread.

Buffalo herd at Taos Pueblo.

handicrafts. Large drums of unusual sonority are made of rawhide stretched over cottonwood or aspen trunks that have been hollowed out by hand. Craftsmen also weave rugs of rabbit skin and make wood carvings, jewelry, and pottery.

Today a number of Taos residents have jobs off the reservation; many work in the nearby town of Taos. However, the lives of the people still center around the spiritual and ceremonial practices of the pueblo, which are solidly anchored in religious traditions of the past. These traditions are very old; archaeological evidence found at the pueblo suggests that these religious beliefs and rituals evolved elsewhere and were brought to Taos when it was first settled. The religious beliefs and ceremonial rituals of the Taos Indians are concerned with man's place in the universe, and his function in controlling and propitiating natural forces, such as weather, plants, and animals. Man's role in maintaining order is also related to the restoration, through healing, of the balance of forces gone awry.

Wood carving and many other traditional crafts are passed down in families, from generation to generation.

Julia Montoya makes ceramic dolls.

Leandro Bernal making moccasins from deerskin.

Teresino Jiron is famous for his drum making, and people from all over the world buy his drums.

Although there is a small Catholic church at the pueblo, where the people of Taos attend services, their Christian beliefs have not supplanted the original belief system, but simply coexist alongside it. The Taos Indians believe in a harmony between man and nature in which man is merely one part of the totality of nature. Although they love the Christian deities and saints, they have an equally deep affection for nature deities, particularly those directly concerned with their sustenance: the Corn Mother; the Squash Maidens; the rain gods, who bring life-giving moisture; and the hunting gods, who help them locate food.

Many of the ancient agricultural practices required communal cooperation, and they still serve to build a sense of tribal unity today. The scarcity of water led to small-scale hydraulic works, requiring people to work together digging ditches, building dams, terracing, and clearing; cooperation was necessary in order to schedule the distribution of the water supply. Other large-scale activities, like livestock raising and corn harvesting, also require group participation, if only among members of the extended family.

In the traditional view of the Taos Indians, there is essentially no difference between man's relations with nature, his relations with fellow men, and his relations with the higher powers. There is simply one law, that of interdependence. The maintenance of order is dependent upon man's relations with the spiritual world, with his fellow men, and with the natural world.

Traditional Taos religious celebrations begin and end in the kiva, an underground

ceremonial chamber. There are six kivas at Taos, maintained by six different kiva societies. When a boy reaches the age of ten, he leaves his home to live in a kiva for eighteen months, undergoing various types of training and initiations to complete his religious education. Only men and boys participate in these rituals.

There is no electricity in certain parts of the pueblo, so Taos families eat by the light of a kerosene lamp.

Ladders are used for the traditional two-story Taos Pueblo architecture.

Many families keep horses at Taos Pueblo.

It is traditional for the men of the pueblo to wear
blankets year-round and women shawls.

Winter is the season for grandparents to tell
stories to the grandchildren around the fireplace.

The most completely communal activities at Taos Pueblo are the great festival dances. One of the most famous, held either on Christmas Day or on January 6, is the Deer Dance of Taos, in which throngs of "deer" are led by a "deer maiden." The Buffalo and Deer Dances are held in the winter. The Corn Dances are held in the spring and summer and are also well known. Other striking and memorable events include the Turtle Dance held on New Year's Day, the Christmas Procession, and the fall fiesta and relay race.

Blue Lake

SINCE WATER, agriculture, and livestock are important to the Taos people, it is clear that Blue Lake, the source of the pueblo's water supply, is of great significance to the pueblo, for practical as well as symbolic reasons. In practical terms Blue Lake is the source of life for Taos; but this image has a higher meaning that includes spiritual as well as physical sustenance. According to the beliefs of the Taos Indians, the source from which we emerge is also the source to which we return. Thus symbolically Blue Lake is also the repository for the souls of the departed Taos people.

For centuries, one of the most sacred of all Taos ceremonies was the annual pilgrimage to Blue Lake. The twenty-mile journey took two days on horseback, and the time at the lake was spent in dances and ceremonies whose content and meaning have never been revealed to outsiders. Not even the repression by Spanish missionaries ruptured the annual Blue Lake rituals.

"It seems, when you go up there to Blue Lake, you thank God for the lake, which is blue like turquoise stone. It is twenty miles and takes two days by horseback. It gives me a feeling of being closer to the Spirit and Nature. When it is time to come home, I want to thank God."
—Reyesita Bernal

However, in 1906, when Blue Lake and the surrounding lands were taken from the Taos Indians by the United States Government and made part of what would become Carson National Forest, the ancient traditions were seriously threatened. Originally, the Indians did not protest this seizure because they believed it would serve to protect their sacred land from commercialization. But very soon roads were built into the wilderness, and sacred lands were desecrated by loggers, hunters and campers. Indians who had left prayer sticks, wooden paddles decorated with feathers and symbols, in the fields or woods around Blue Lake often found that the prayer sticks had been removed or destroyed. Following this, the Indians began to take steps to secure Blue Lake's return to their own control.

After some time, the United States Indian Claims Commission confirmed the legitimacy of the Indians' request. In 1926, the United States Government, acting through the commission, offered to pay $297,684.67 to the Indians for the land taken from them. The land under discussion at that time consisted of a 50,000-acre parcel that included Blue Lake and the surrounding wilderness, as well as a much larger parcel comprising all the land in and around what is now the town of Taos. Over the years a number of people had settled on Indian land and built up the town known as Don Fernando de Taos (now shortened to "Taos"). They occupied much of the richest valley

49

land that originally belonged to the pueblo; the total Indian land appropriated by non-Indians exceeded 130,000 acres.

The Indian Claims Commission had the authority to award financial compensation, but not to return the land, and the Taos Indians did not want money; all they wanted was clear title to the sacred Blue Lake area. In order to achieve this, they agreed to give up all rights and titles to the land in and around the town of Taos, if only their Blue Lake land could be returned. Their offer to renounce claims to the town of Taos was immediately accepted, but Blue Lake was not returned.

After a delay of seven years, Congress passed an act in 1933 giving the Indians a fifty-year special use permit. This permit granted Taos Pueblo the right to occupy land around Blue Lake and use its resources for the benefit of the tribe. But this victory was incomplete, and the arrangement failed when the United States Forest Service allowed public recreation in the area shortly thereafter. Four access trails were cut to the lake, and it was stocked with trout, which fishermen sometimes caught with dynamite. The area was opened for camping, and an "administrative center" with open trash pits was built on the edge of the lake. Once again the Indians' privacy was invaded and their sacred site defiled. In 1961, Governor Seferino Martinez and Secretary Paul Bernal of Taos began to lead a vigorous pueblo campaign for full title to Blue Lake. Attorneys for the Association of American Indian Affairs looked into official records. Newspapers across the country carried editorials backing the tribe's claim to Blue Lake and to their religious freedom.

Four years later, the Indian Claims Commission ruled that the Taos people had been unjustly deprived of their property. Again it offered the only recompense it was empowered to provide: $297,684.67. Again the Indians refused. "We will not sell our religion, our life," they proclaimed.

An unexpected ally was the National Council of Churches, which, in support of the Indian cause, pointed out the correspondences between sacred structures like cathedrals and mosques and the Blue Lake region. The council said, "What the Indians of Taos Pueblo are asking is that equal consideration, no more, no less, be extended to the shrine where they have performed their religious obligations for at least as long as the famed cathedrals of Europe have been in use."

Between 1966 and 1969, five bills were introduced in Congress to settle the Blue Lake issue. Objections were raised by the United States Forest Service, which was willing to release to the Indians the barren rocks of the western slope, but wanted to retain as large a portion as possible of the fertile eastern slope with its springs and valuable timber. This effort followed the long-standing pattern of United States Government dealings with Indians, in which the government allocated to the Indians land it did not want.

A principal conflict arose from differences between Indian and

government conceptions of the Blue Lake region's value. To the Indians, not just the lake, but all that surrounded it was sacred. The animals and plants, as well as the earth itself were seen as living creatures whose integrity was intimately bound up with that of the tribe. The Indians called the Blue Lake trees "living saints" and felt that a tree, if cut, would bleed; the United States Forest Service believed that an uncut tree was profit potential going to waste. The Indians had long visited some of the high meadows to search for food or for medicinal and ritual plants, or to clean springs for the deer that came there to drink. These activities were accompanied by prayer and a deep appreciation of all living beings. The United States Forest Service viewed the high meadows as useful commercial grazing lands and had charged rent for their use by cattle ranchers. As a result, the springs were muddied, the deer were driven deep into the woods, and the food and medicinal plants were depleted.

Testifying while he was governor of Taos Pueblo, Quirino Romero said, "I am hurt in my heart the way we have to fight for our sacred land, the way we have to fight for this burial land, on which we have been brought up, the land that we have traveled to pray to our spirit of God, to pray to God in our own way."

Juan de Jesús Romero, tribal cacique, stated, "Our Blue Lake wilderness keeps our water holy, and by the water we are baptized. If our land is not returned to us, if it is turned over to the government for its use, then that is the end of Indian life. Our people will scatter as the people of other nations have scattered. It is our religion that holds us together."

During the hearings, the Taos Indians remarked that they would accept 48,000 of the 50,000 acres, providing the other 2,000 acres would be put into the wilderness area that the government had created adjoining their land. With support building on all sides, a decisive blow was struck by President Richard Nixon when, in his July 8, 1970, message to Congress, he called the Blue Lake claim "an important symbol of government's responsiveness to the just grievances of all American Indians."

Finally, on December 2, 1970, at the close of a two-day debate, the Senate voted 70 to 12 to return to Taos Pueblo Blue Lake and the surrounding land taken from it sixty-five years earlier. The longest battle fought by the Taos Indians had been won at last. This conflict, whose outcome was perhaps the most critical of all to their survival, had been won with no bloodshed.

President Nixon signed the bill into law on December 15, 1970. The news of success was announced at Taos on the mission bell. As the people gathered, crying and laughing, the ninety-year-old Caci-

que Juan de Jesús Romero spoke for all when he said, "We are going to enjoy a happy New Year every year!"

The Blue Lake victory ceremony that followed on August 14 and 15, 1971, was the most joyous celebration seen at Taos Pueblo in a very long time. Prayers of thanksgiving, songs, dances, speeches, and a buffalo feast marked the event. The celebration was open to the public, and non-Indians who had particularly helped the tribe regain its land were honored. These included Secretary of the Interior Rogers C. B. Morton and former Secretary of the Interior Stewart L. Udall; Senator Fred Harris of Oklahoma; Senator Robert Griffin of Michigan; United States Representative Manuel Lujan, Jr.; and former New Mexico Governor David F. Cargo. But when Paul Bernal, who had served as secretary to the Taos Pueblo Council for twenty-four years, and who had fought unceasingly for Blue Lake for many years, was asked who had led the battle from Taos, he said, "No one man. All together. The governor, the council, all the people."

The return of Blue Lake to Taos Pueblo has set a precedent for Indian nations throughout the country. As a result of this legislation, many other tribes who had not received compensation for, or return of, unjustly seized lands have demanded redress. Some of them have already received compensation, and legal action has also been undertaken to return to the tribes sacred relics, implements, and ancestral bones from museums and other collections.

Taos Pueblo celebrates the victory of the return of
Blue Lake, August 1971.

Feathered lances, placed upright in the ground, symbolized the victory of the Taos Indians in regaining their sacred Blue Lake.

A memorable victory celebration was held in 1971 to give thanks for the return of Blue Lake. The celebration began with a parade through the pueblo. Children danced with bells tied to their feet, and the tinkling sound blended with haunting Indian chants and the rhythmic throb of drums.

At Taos Pueblo people of all ages danced all day long in celebration.

According to the late Juan de Jesús Romero, former religious leader of Taos Pueblo, "Our Blue Lake wilderness keeps our water holy, and by the water we are baptized. If our land is not returned to us, if it is turned over to the government for its use, then that is the end of Indian life. Our people will scatter as the people of other nations have scattered. It is our religion that holds us together."

The Future

TWENTY YEARS have passed since the return of Blue Lake to its rightful owners. Some things have not changed at Taos Pueblo: those who dwell in the adobe apartment buildings on either side of the central plaza still live, as they prefer to do, without electricity or running water. However, now the water of the Rio Pueblo, in the center of the plaza, is clean and pure.

High above the plaza, pristine in its mountain setting, Blue Lake is once again a sacred site. During the last twenty years, the elders of Taos Pueblo who had only remembered the ceremonies of their youth, and young people who had never even experienced them, have joined together regularly at Blue Lake to celebrate the mysteries surrounding the origin and spiritual home of their people. Wildflowers, wild asparagus, and medicinal plants grow once more in the high meadows, and deer graze freely and drink from clear pools.

At the Blue Lake victory celebration, Taos Pueblo Governor John Reyna said that the triumph "came to be by the efforts not only of our own people but of others who were interested in preserving our way of life, those who, even though they don't understand what our way of life is, know it is valuable and ought to be preserved."

Now, twenty years after those remarks, many more people have come to understand the value of the Indian way of life, and that understanding promises to benefit all of society. At the same time, Pueblo Indian society has proved to be immensely hardy, capable of development and growth even while it is fighting to keep its old traditions alive and its secrets intact. There is no doubt that Taos Pueblo will endure and flourish, and, in doing so, will provide inspiration for other native peoples to reclaim their spiritual heritage. These collective wisdoms, the living traditions of our native peoples, whether closely guarded or widely disseminated, enrich the spiritual fabric of our entire nation.